Knock, Knock Jokes for Kids

Earl Edwards

ISBN-10:1492145521
ISBN-13:9781492145523

Knock, knock.
Who's there?
Walter.
Walter who?
Walter you doin today?

Knock, knock.
Who's there?
T-Rex.
T-Rex who?
You mean there is a T-Rex at your door
and you want to know his name?

Knock, knock.
Who's there?
Bark.
Bark who?
Barak Obama

Knock, knock.
Who's there?
Ketchup.
Ketchup who?
Ketchup with you soon!

Knock, knock.
Who's there?
Ice cream soda.
Ice cream soda who?
Ice cream soda you can come open the
door

Knock, knock.
Who's there?
Adore.
Adore who?
Adore is between us! Open up!

Knock, knock.
Who's there?
Amos.
Amos who?
A mosquito bit me

Knock, knock.
Who's there?
Anita.
Anita who?
Anita nother minute to think it over.

WELL WELL WELL
WHAT DO WE HAVE HERE ?

Knock, knock.
Who's there?
Tank.
Tank who?
Tank you!

Knock, knock.
Who's there?
Courtney.
Courtney who?
Courtney thieves lately?

Knock, knock.
Who's there?
Lego.
Lego who?
Lego of me and I'll tell ya!

Knock, knock.
Who's there?
Owls.
Owl who?
Owl you doing today?

Knock, knock.
Who's there?
Alfred.
Alfred who?
Alfred you won't open the door!

Knock, knock.
Who's there
Kanga.
Kanga who?
No, kanga-roo!

Knock, knock.
Who's there?
Who.
Who who?
Is there an owl in here?

Knock, knock.
Who's there!
Bark!
Bark who?
Bark you car on the drive!

Knock, knock.
Who's there?
Beggar.
Beggar who?
It's Beggar you don't know!

Knock, knock.
Who's there?
Bison.
Bison who?
Bison girl scout cookies!

Knock, knock.
Who's there?
Repeat.
Repeat who?
Who who who who who who

Knock, knock.
Who's There?
Ashe.
Ashe who?
Bless you!

Knock, knock.
Who's there?
Nobel.
Nobel who?
No bell, that's why I knocked!

Knock, knock.
Who's there?
Leaf.
Leaf who?
Leaf me alone!

Knock, knock.
Who's There?
Lettuce.
Lettuce who?
Lettuce in and you'll find out!

Knock-knock
Who's there?
Aaron.
Aaron who?
Why Aaron you opening the door?

Knock, knock.
Who's there?
Hawaii.
Hawaii who?
I'm fine, Hawaii you?

Knock, knock.
Who's there?
Orange.
Orange who?
Orange you even going to open the door?

Knock, knock.
Who's There?
Anita.
Anita who?
Anita to borrow a pencil.

Knock, knock.
Who's There?
Woo.
Woo who?
Don't get so excited, it's just a joke.

AMERICAN
AVIATION
LEARN TO
FLY HERE!

Knock, knock.
Who's There?
Figs.
Figs who?
Figs the doorbell, it's broken!

Knock-knock
Who's there?
Alice.
Alice who?
Alice fair in love and war.

Knock, knock.
Who's There?
Annie.
Annie Who?
Annie time I knock on the door
you never answer!

Knock-knock
Who's there?
Yukon.
Yukon who?
Yukon say that again!

Knock, knock.
Who's There?
Theodore.
Theodore who?
Theodore is stuck and it won't open!

Knock, knock.
Who's there?
Cash.
Cash who?
No thanks, but I would like a peanut
instead!

Knock, knock.
Who's there?
Doris.
Doris who
Doris locked, that's why I'm knocking!

Knock, knock.
Who's there?
Banana.
Banana who?
Knock, knock.
Who's there?
Banana.
Banana who?
Knock, knock.
Who's there?
Banana.
Banana who?
Knock, knock.
Who's there?
Orange.
Orange who?
Orange you glad I didn't say "banana"?

Knock, knock.
Who's there?
Interrupting cow.
Interrupt-MOOOOOOOOOOOOOOO!!
(Say "moo" as soon as they start to reply)

Timon and Pumbaa?!

Knock, knock.
Who's there?
Honey bee.
Honey bee who?
Honey be a deer and get me a soda!

Knock, knock.
Who's there?
Madam.
Madam who?
Madam foot got caught in the door!

Knock, knock.
Who's there?
Me.
Me who?
No, seriously, it's just me.
I am telling a Knock, knock. joke.

Knock, knock.
Who's there?
Cows go.
Cows go who?
No, cows go moo!

Knock, knock.
Who's there?
Oink oink.
Oink oink who?
Make up your mind; are you a pig or an
owl?!

Knock, knock.
Who's there?
Barbie.
Barbie Who?
Barbie Q Chicken!

Knock, knock.
Who's there?
Kiwi.
Kiwi who?
Kiwi go to the store?

Knock, knock.
Who's there?
Lettuce.
Lettuce who?
Let us in, we're freezing!

Knock, knock.
Who's there?
Olive.
Olive who?
Olive right next door to you.

Knock, knock.
Who's there?
Turnip.
Turnip who?
Turnip the volume I like that song!

Knock, knock.
Who's there?
Ice cream
Ice cream who?
Ice cream if you don't let me in!

Knock, knock.
Who's there?
Orange.
Orange who?
Orange you going to answer the door?

FIAT
I FEEL PRETTY
Oh, so pretty

Knock, knock.
Who's there?
Orange.
Orange who?
Orange you glad to see me?

Knock, knock.
Who's there?
Cow-go.
Cow-go who?
No, Cow go MOO!

Knock, knock.
Who's there?
Police.
Police who?
Police (please) may I come in?

Knock, knock.
Who's there?
Water.
Water who?
Water you doing in my house?

Knock, knock.
Who's there?
Goat.
Goat who?
Goat to the door and find out.

Knock, knock.
Who's there?
Beef.
Beef who?
Before I get cold, you'd better let me in!

Knock, knock.
Who's there?
Duane.
Duane who?
Duane the tub! I'm done with my bath.

Knock, knock.
Who's there?
Abe Lincoln.
Abe Lincoln who?
Don't you know who Abe Lincoln is?

Knock, knock.
Who's there?
Handsome.
Handsome who?
Handsome cookies to me and I'll tell you

Knock, knock.
Who's there?
Cow.
Cow who?
No! Cows go Moo!

Knock, knock.
Who's there?
Ach-hoo.
Ach-hoo who?
Bless you!

Knock, knock.
Who's there?
Cargo.
Cargo who?
No, a car goes beep beep!

Knock, knock.
Who's there?
Warrior.
Warrior who?
Warrior been all my life!

Knock, knock.
Who's there?
Police.
Police who?
Police! Open up!

Knock, knock.
Who's there?
Anna Mary.
Anna Mary who?
Anna Mary old sole was he!

Knock, knock.
Who's there?
Anita.
Anita who?
Anita get in this house

Knock, knock.
Who's there?
Olive.
Olive who?
Olive you!

Knock, knock.
Who's there?
Lettuce.
Lettuce who?
Lettuce in it's cold outside!

Knock, knock.
Who's there?
I Love.
I Love who?
I don't know, you tell me!

Knock, knock.
Who's there?
Who.
Who who?
I didn't know you were an owl!

PATIENT BEAR
Will be ready when you are

Knock, knock.
Who's there?
Sherwood.
Sherwood who?
Sherwood like to come in!

Knock, knock.
Who's there?
Wa.
Wa who?
Boy you are really excited to see me!!

Knock, knock.
Who's there?
I am.
I am who?
You don't know who you are?

Knock, knock.
Who's there?
Owl.
Owl who?
That's right - owls who!

Knock, knock.
Who's there?
A little boy.
A little boy who?
A little boy who can't reach the doorbell.

Knock, knock.
Who's there?
Hutch.
Hutch who?
Bless you!!!

Knock, knock.
Who's there?
Tank.
Tank who?
You're welcome!

Knock, knock.
Who's there?
Goliath.
Goliath who?
Goliath down, you look sleepy!!

Knock, knock.
Who's there?
Old Lady.
Old lady who?
I didn't know you could yodel!

Knock, knock.
Who's there?
Ivana.
Ivana who?
Ivana come in!

Knock, knock.
Who's there?
Teresa.
Teresa who?
Trees are green!

Knock, knock.
Who's there?
Stew.
Stew who?
Stew early to go to bed

Knock, knock.
Who's there?
Good morning to.
Good morning to who?
Good morning to you silly goose!

Knock, knock.
Who's there?
Courtney.
Courtney who?
Courtney criminals yet?

Knock, knock.
Who's there?
Tom.
Tom who?
Tom Ate Toe!

Knock, knock.
Who's there?
Who.
Who who?
You sound like an owl!

Knock, knock.
Who's there?
Philip.
Philip who?
Philip my cup, I'm really thirsty

Knock, knock.
Who's there?
Abby.
Abby who?
Abby Birthday to you!

Knock, knock.
Who's there?
Mango.
Mango who?
Man-go get someone to open the door

Knock, knock.
Who's there?
Andy.
Andy who?
Andy day now, Andy day now

Knock, knock.
Who's there?
Jermain.
Jermain who?
Jermain you don't remember me?

Knock, knock.
Who's there?
Ketchup.
Ketchup Who?
Didn't I already say, Ketchup!

Knock, knock.
Who's there?
Oprah.
Oprah Who?
Oprah Winfrey! Duh!

Knock, knock.
Who's there?
Issac.
Issac Who?
Issac (I sick) of Knock, knock. Jokes!

Knock, knock.
Who's there?
Notta.
Notta who?
Notta nother mosquito!

Knock, knock.
Who's there?
Bart.
Bart who?
Bart time you open the door

Knock, knock.
Who's there?
Dishes.
Dishes who?
Dishes your friend. Open the door

Knock, knock.
Who's there?
Hairy.
Hairy who?
Hairy up and let us in!

A TRIP TO THE VET
He's Gonna Stick That Thermometer Where ?

Knock, knock.
Who's there?
Donut.
Donut who?
Donut Run when you get the door

Knock, knock.
Who's there?
Maya.
Maya who?
Maya name is............

Knock, knock.
Who's there?
Owl.
Owl who?
Owl you doing today?

Knock, knock.
Who's there?
Jimmie.
Jimmie who?
Jimmie your money because
I need it more than you.

Knock, knock.
Who's there?
Crab.
Crab who?
Crab me a Sandwich!

Knock, knock.
Who's there?
Owls.
Owls who?
You're right! Owls DO hoo!

Knock, knock.
Who's there?
Phyllis.
Phyllis who?
Phyllis a glass of water please!

Knock, knock.
Who's there?
Armageddon.
Armageddon who?
Armageddon outta here!!

Knock, knock.
Who's there?
Lego.
Lego who?
Lego my eggo!!

Knock, knock.
Who's there?
Simon says.
Simon says Who?
Who who who who who who who

Knock, knock.
Who's there?
Justin Bieber.
Justin Beiber Who?
You don't know who Justin Bieber is?

Knock, knock.
Who's there?
Needle.
Needle who?
I need a little money rite now!

Knock, knock.
Who's there?
Oink.
Oink who?
Could you please make up your mind
are you a pig or a cow!

Knock, knock.
Who's there?
Justin.
Justin who?
Justin time for dinner!

Knock, knock.
Who's there?
Kenya.
Kenya who?
Kenya please open up the door?

Knock, knock.
Who's there?
Warrior.
Warrior who?
Warrior been all day

Knock, knock.
Who's there?
Honey bee.
Honey bee who?
Honey be a dear and get me a snack

Knock, knock.
Who's there?
Ivan.
Ivan who?
Ivana go to the bathroom

Knock, knock.
Who's there?
I don't know.
I don't know who
I just told you I don't know!

Knock, knock.
Who's there?
Police.
Police who?
Police open the door!